Heal Your Past & Live Today

33 Daily Affirmations to Heal Your Soul

AILEEN CASTELLANO

D1468674

FREE GIFT FOR MY READERS

As a way of saying THANK YOU to my Readers I have a special gift for you.

Sign up for your FREE 45-minute Call with me to "Break Free from the Fear and Anxiety that are Keeping You Stuck".

We don't often know what is keeping us blocked or stuck, this call will help uncover those unconscious blocks.

Book Your Call NOW:
https://www.aileenc.com

About Aileen Castellano

Aileen Castellano is a Wealthness Coach, Spiritual Entrepreneur, Ascension Mentor, Speaker, and Self-Development Author with over 17 years of experience as a Marriage and Family Therapist and Mediator. Before she began helping clients with life changing transitions, Aileen excelled in the world of finance and banking, expanded her family's construction business, and became an executive recruiter for a fortune 500 company. Later, she obtained a master's degree in marriage and family therapy, and during her nearly two decades in private practice, served as a Florida Supreme Court certified mediator.

Aileen is the founder of Famwell Healing, creator of the *Sacred Surrender Program*, and developer of the *Guide to Wealthness*. She teaches people all over the world the practice of meditation with intention, incorporating crystal healing modalities. Her vast knowledge of therapeutic practices, karmic healing, past life regressions, and energy healing techniques set her apart in the coaching field. Her life's work and passion have helped her step into purpose to blend practices, beliefs, and mantras that result in life-changing experiences and empowering modalities that make a profound and powerful impact on clients. Her passion to inspire has afforded her the opportunity to live out a dreams-fulfilled life.

Dedication

To my beautiful children Michael, Daniel, Katrina, and Gabriel for being the light in my life that inspired me to continue looking forward to creating the life of my dreams. I love you more than you'll ever know.

Lots of love and light.

Table of Contents

Introduction

I was inspired to write this book because after many years of working with clients of various ages and backgrounds, I realized how much we're all stuck in the hurtful experiences of the past. During these sessions, it became evident that for most people, the process of letting go was detrimental; healing was the only way to move forward with life.

As the recorder of all the different events in someone's life, the subconscious mind holds the information at a soul level. Therefore, we must introduce positive thoughts to replace the old, worn ways of thinking through a daily practice of mantras or affirmations. This is where the reprogramming takes place and initiates healing at every level. It has been life-changing to witness the impact of new thoughts on another person; for it is only when we embrace the opportunity presented to us to release the past that stepping into our purpose becomes a reality.

A daily practice of mantras or affirmations is vital for consistency and maintenance of the positive thoughts flooding the mind. It becomes a new way of living where positivity holds a higher consciousness, while the lower-vibrating thoughts begin to dissipate and disappear. At that point, the heart begins to open and connects to passion – the driving force behind living a life of purpose. In the process of holding positive thoughts, your intentions become more clear and powerful. The alignment of the high consciousness of positive thoughts, healed emotions, and high vibrational energy combine to attract and manifest your desired reality. It makes the process of manifesting easier and more deliberate. I know that applying this daily practice will enhance your thoughts and raise your energetic vibration to align you with all you want to attract into your life.

How to Use This Book

*Practice silencing your mind and
you can hear the whispers of your soul.*

This book has been written for you to begin the process of releasing the old pattern of thoughts and behaviors that have kept you stuck in certain areas of your life. As you let go of what doesn't serve you, the affirmation will help replace it with new thoughts and perspectives. The magical experience of releasing the old and replacing it with the new creates a profound shift in your old patterns and helps you to step into a new reality.

I recommend that you go through one release and affirmation each day. If you feel you need to process any one release and affirmation for a few more days before moving onto the next one, give yourself permission to do just that. Pause and reflect upon what you want to let go and what you want to expand in your life. For best results, use the available space to write about any feelings or thoughts that come up.

There are inspirational quotes at the top of each page to help you navigate your journey through healing and manifesting the new experience of a dreams-fulfilled life. It is precious. Live yours to its fullest!

Heal Your Past
& Live Today

33 Daily Affirmations
to Heal Your Soul

1

Have the courage to leave behind that which blocks you from living a life you love.

Release

Today, I release all the negative triggers from other people's words or actions that affect me.

Affirmation

I choose to fill my heart with peace and joy, today and every day.

Reflections

_____

_____

_____

_____

_____

_____

_____

_____

_____

_____

_____

_____

_____

_____

_____

_____

_____

_____

2

Choose peace over being right.

Release

Today, I release the need to be right or prove myself to others.

Affirmation

I choose to allow the flow of blessings into my life with ease and grace.

Reflections

_____

_____

_____

_____

_____

_____

_____

_____

_____

_____

_____

_____

_____

_____

_____

_____

_____

_____

_____

3

No one can ever know your visions as you do, so stay inspired to follow your dreams despite what they think.

Release

Today, I release the need to engage in drama with others.

Affirmation

I choose to see the goodness in everyone around me.

Reflections

_____
_____
_____
_____
_____
_____
_____
_____
_____
_____
_____
_____
_____
_____
_____
_____
_____
_____
_____
_____

4

Find peace in the chaos of your life.

Release

Today, I release myself from the feelings of over-whelm and anxiety.

Affirmation

I choose to enjoy every breath I take.

Reflections

_____

_____

_____

_____

_____

_____

_____

_____

_____

_____

_____

_____

_____

_____

_____

_____

_____

_____

_____

5

Surrender to the message within; your soul already knows what's best.

Release

Today, I let go of over-thinking and worry.

Affirmation

I choose to silence my mind and focus on something beautiful in nature.

Reflections

_____

_____

_____

_____

_____

_____

_____

_____

_____

_____

_____

_____

_____

_____

_____

_____

_____

_____

6

Surrender, allow, and accept that it is all in divine order.

Release

Today, I release fearfulness of what is to come.

Affirmation

I choose to embrace and surrender to all that is already here.

Reflections

7

*Find the perfection in the imperfections
and you will find peace.*

Release

Today, I release the need to notice qualities in myself
that I don't like.

Affirmation

I choose to see how amazing and beautiful I really
am.

Reflections

_____

_____

_____

_____

_____

_____

_____

_____

_____

_____

_____

_____

_____

_____

_____

_____

_____

_____

_____

8

You can't change anyone; you can only embrace their individuality.

Release

Today, I release the anger I project on those I love.

Affirmation

I choose to use kind words when talking to the special people in my life.

Reflections

9

Love your life today.

Release

Today, I release the buildup of old issues that disrupt my peace of mind.

Affirmation

I choose to live in the present moment of joy.

Reflections

_____

_____

_____

_____

_____

_____

_____

_____

_____

_____

_____

_____

_____

_____

_____

_____

_____

_____

_____

_____

10

The light is yours; don't give it away.

Release

Today, I release the need to be a victim of the actions of others.

Affirmation

I choose to take my power back by feeling strong and moving toward my life's goals.

Reflections

11

Release yourself from darkness and connect to the light.

Release

Today, I release the need to feel sorry for myself.

Affirmation

I choose to feel free to be whoever and whatever I want.

Reflections

12

Surrender, allow and accept as you feel serene and peaceful.

Release

Today, I release the sorrow of losing someone or something that was special to me.

Affirmation

I choose to honor and embrace the memories of having them in my life.

Reflections

13

You are perfectly where you are, right here and right now.

Release

Today, I release all regrets about what could have been.

Affirmation

I choose to live in the moment of all I am creating, right here and right now.

Reflections

_____
_____
_____
_____
_____
_____
_____
_____
_____
_____
_____
_____
_____
_____
_____
_____
_____
_____
_____
_____
_____
_____
_____

14

When you awaken, you realize it's all perfect.

Release

Today, I release the feeling that I must have it all in this moment.

Affirmation

I choose to surrender, allow the process, and enjoy the journey.

Reflections

15

When you think of the worst you attract the worst. When you think of the best you attract the best. You choose the reality you want to experience.

Release

Today, I release the thought that something bad is going to happen.

Affirmation

I choose to know that everything always works out for the best.

Reflections

_____

_____

_____

_____

_____

_____

_____

_____

_____

_____

_____

_____

_____

_____

_____

_____

_____

_____

16

If you fall in love with you, you will attract your true love.

Release

Today, I release the fear of being alone for the rest of my life.

Affirmation

I choose to believe that the perfect partner is on their way to me.

Reflections

_____

_____

_____

_____

_____

_____

_____

_____

_____

_____

_____

_____

_____

_____

_____

_____

_____

_____

_____

_____

17

*Embrace the love within you
and feel your light radiate.*

Release

Today, I release the buildup of old emotions that have kept me stuck in the past.

Affirmation

I choose to embrace new emotions of love and peace.

Reflections

18

I allow that which no longer serves me to leave my life as I bless and let it go.

Release

Today, I release the heartache of being betrayed and rejected.

Affirmation

I choose to heal my heart and believe that I can trust again.

Reflections

_____

_____

_____

_____

_____

_____

_____

_____

_____

_____

_____

_____

_____

_____

_____

_____

_____

_____

_____

_____

_____

19

Align to the energy of unconditional love and you will find bliss.

Release

Today, I release all the moments when I have felt abandoned and dismissed.

Affirmation

I choose to feel acknowledged and special.

Reflections

_____
_____
_____
_____
_____
_____
_____
_____
_____
_____
_____
_____
_____
_____
_____
_____
_____
_____
_____
_____
_____
_____
_____

20

*Connect to your purpose and find
the beat to the music of your heart.*

Release

Today, I release all thoughts of not being good
enough.

Affirmation

I choose to feel that I am more than good enough.

Reflections

_____

_____

_____

_____

_____

_____

_____

_____

_____

_____

_____

_____

_____

_____

_____

_____

_____

_____

_____

21

Today is the perfect day to start something new.

Release

Today, I release thoughts of judgment.

Affirmation

I choose to be free to be myself.

Reflections

_____
_____
_____
_____
_____
_____
_____
_____
_____
_____
_____
_____
_____
_____
_____
_____
_____
_____
_____
_____
_____

22

Savor each breath of life deliciously.

Release

Today, I release bitterness from my heart.

Affirmation

I choose to allow sweetness and gentleness to support me.

Reflections

_____

_____

_____

_____

_____

_____

_____

_____

_____

_____

_____

_____

_____

_____

_____

_____

_____

_____

_____

_____

_____

23

It's all in the flow of awesomeness.

Release

Today, I release staying stuck in the past.

Affirmation

I choose to be in the moment right now.

Reflections

_____

_____

_____

_____

_____

_____

_____

_____

_____

_____

_____

_____

_____

_____

_____

_____

_____

_____

_____

_____

_____

24

Reflect on who you really are and keep the essence that defines you.

Release

Today, I release seeing myself small and insignificant.

Affirmation

I choose to see the greatness within me.

Reflections

_____

_____

_____

_____

_____

_____

_____

_____

_____

_____

_____

_____

_____

_____

_____

_____

_____

_____

_____

_____

25

*We create that which affects us,
so create that which fills you with bliss.*

Release

Today, I release the need to surround myself with people who drain my energy.

Affirmation

I choose to be around people who elevate me.

Reflections

_____

_____

_____

_____

_____

_____

_____

_____

_____

_____

_____

_____

_____

_____

_____

_____

_____

_____

_____

_____

_____

26

Surrender into your new journey.

Release

Today, I release past experiences that filled me with sorrow and fear.

Affirmation

I choose to accept the perfection in what happened to lead me to this very day.

Reflections

_____

_____

_____

_____

_____

_____

_____

_____

_____

_____

_____

_____

_____

_____

_____

_____

_____

_____

_____

_____

27

Create a life you love.

Release

Today, I release feeling like a victim and making excuses for myself.

Affirmation

I choose to take responsibility, so that I can own my life and fulfill my dreams.

Reflections

28

Change the way you do things, so that your outcomes are different.

Release

Today, I release all the times I was stubborn and stuck.

Affirmation

I choose to be flexible and open to everything in my life today.

Reflections

_____

_____

_____

_____

_____

_____

_____

_____

_____

_____

_____

_____

_____

_____

_____

_____

_____

_____

_____

_____

29

Be true to your essence.

Release

Today, I release my demands to have things as I want them.

Affirmation

I choose to surrender and accept God's plan, which offers more that I can ever imagine.

Reflections

_____

_____

_____

_____

_____

_____

_____

_____

_____

_____

_____

_____

_____

_____

_____

_____

_____

_____

_____

_____

_____

_____

30

Shine the light from within you.

Release

Today, I release all the tears I have cried for everyone who has disappointed me.

Affirmation

I choose to forgive them and myself, to open my heart to giving and receiving love.

Reflections

_____

_____

_____

_____

_____

_____

_____

_____

_____

_____

_____

_____

_____

_____

_____

_____

_____

_____

_____

_____

_____

_____

31

Align Your Purpose to the REAL YOU.

Release

Today, I release the karma I created by not listening to my inner wisdom.

Affirmation

I choose to connect to my Higher Self for guidance in manifesting a life of joy.

Reflections

_____
_____
_____
_____
_____
_____
_____
_____
_____
_____
_____
_____
_____
_____
_____
_____
_____
_____
_____
_____
_____

32

You are All of YOUR Lifetimes.

Release

Today, I release all the trauma I have carried from my past lives and current life.

Affirmation

I choose to heal and bring forth all the beautiful gifts from all my lifetimes.

Reflections

_____

_____

_____

_____

_____

_____

_____

_____

_____

_____

_____

_____

_____

_____

_____

_____

_____

_____

_____

_____

33

We came to have it all.
Be free to be the best that you can be.

Release

Today, I release my old consciousness, which holds me in lower vibrations.

Affirmation

I choose to step into Christ consciousness, living in the high vibrational energy connected to the Crystalline Grid.

Reflections

_____

_____

_____

_____

_____

_____

_____

_____

_____

_____

_____

_____

_____

_____

_____

_____

_____

_____

_____

_____

_____

_____

Made in the USA
Middletown, DE
11 January 2020